The LMS Story

The LMS Story

David Wragg

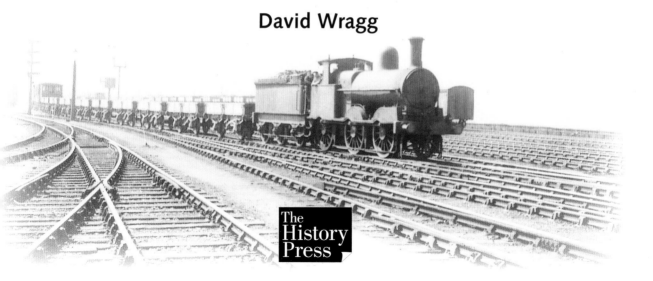

The
History
Press

Published in the United Kingdom in 2013 by
The History Press
The Mill · Brimscombe Port · Stroud · Gloucestershire · GL5 2QG

British Library Cataloguing in Publication Data
A catalogue record for this book is available from the British
Library.

Hardback ISBN 978-0-7524-8805-9

Typesetting and origination by The History Press
Printed in India
Manufacturing managed by Jellyfish Solutions Ltd

CONTENTS

Inevitably, in writing a book such as this, I am indebted to the National Railway Museum at York and the vast treasure trove of information contained in its search engine about the old railway companies, their trains and rolling stock, and the people who worked for them. Those in the distant past who compiled and wrote for the *LMS Magazine* also did much to shed light on the workings of the railway. I am also grateful to Sophia Brothers of the Science & Society Picture Library for her kind assistance.

Claimed to be the largest private enterprise concern in the British Empire, the London, Midland & Scottish Railway (LMS) was Britain's largest steam railway and the only one to operate in England, Scotland, Wales and Northern Ireland, as well as having two short stretches of line in the Irish Republic. It was the world's largest owner of railway hotels and the world's largest railway shipping operator. It was mainly a steam railway but had a significant electric service out of Euston in London, and on Merseyside and Manchester, and it was one of the leaders in the introduction of diesel shunting locomotives. It was also a pioneer in using mechanical handling equipment, including large coaling towers.

The LMS was mainly a freight railway, but it boasted the best railway carriages, even on suburban services where there was more legroom than offered by other companies.

The paradox of the LMS, in hindsight, was that while it strove to introduce the most modern management practices, largely imported from the United States, and was at the fore in adopting mechanisation in coaling plants and carriage washing, and even in the construction of railway carriages, it was reluctant to electrify; it saw the steam locomotive as the advanced technology of the day with much potential remaining. In its resistance to change, the LMS continued with many outmoded and costly practices, spurning the concept of what today would be known as liner trains for freight, even when suggested by one of its most important customers.

➤ The sheer enormity of Britain's largest railway company can be seen from this map, with the company operating in England, Scotland, Wales, Northern Ireland and even the Irish Republic. (Bradshaw)

Under Grouping, which saw more than a hundred railway companies merge into just four, the plan was simply to create a 'North Western, Midland and West Scottish' railway company and it took the whole of 1922 for appointments and structures to be agreed; even then, most passengers did not notice the change until 1927, as there was so much to be done. The name chosen was the London, Midland & Scottish Railway, sometimes referred to as the London Midland Scottish, and the abbreviation was always LMS, never LM&S.

As with the other grouped companies – the London & North Eastern Railway (LNER), the Great Western Railway (GWR) and the Southern Railway – the companies absorbed were defined either as constituent companies, which meant they appointed a director on the board of the new company, or subsidiary companies. The London, Midland & Scottish Railway had as its constituent companies the Caledonian Railway; Lancashire & Yorkshire Railway (LYR), which had already agreed to be purchased by the London & North Western Railway (LNWR); Glasgow & South Western Railway; Highland Railway; Midland Railway; North Staffordshire Railway; and the Furness Railway. The subsidiaries included the Arbroath & Forfar Railway; Brechin & Edzell District Railway; Callander & Oban Railway; Cathcart District Railway; Charnwood Forest Railway; Cleator & Workington Junction Railway; Cockermouth, Keswick & Penrith Railway; Dearne Valley Railway; Dornoch Light Railway; Dundee & Newtyle Railway; Harborne Railway; Leek & Manifold Valley Light Railway; Maryport & Carlisle Railway; Mold & Denbigh Junction Railway; North & South Western Junction

➤ The LMS coat of arms, as it would be seen on the side of a passenger carriage. It was not used on locomotives. (Historical Model Railway Society (HMRS))

Railway; North London Railway; Portpatrick & Wigtownshore Joint Committee; Shropshire Union Railways & Canal; Solway Junction Railway; Stratford-upon-Avon & Midland Junction Railway; Tottenham & Forest Gate Railway; Wick & Lynster Light Railway; Wirral Railway; and the Yorkshire Dales Railway.

Some of the smaller lines were already leased to or worked by the larger companies. The Mersey Railway was taken over in 1938 to be absorbed into the LMS's Wirral Lines. The LMS inherited the Midland Railway's share of the Somerset & Dorset Railway, running to the south coast from Bath in partnership with the Southern Railway.

The result of these mergers and acquisitions was a company with 20,000 passenger carriages, 10,000 steam locomotives, 30,000 road vehicles and, before the outbreak of war, more than 70 steamers.

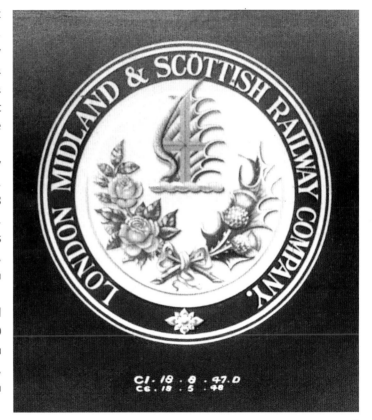

While the LMS was not as conscious of its history as the LNER, for example, care was taken to preserve a number of historic locomotives. This is a former Caledonian Railway 4-2-2 'single-wheeler', still in works grey finish. (HMRS)

Another preserved locomotive was this ex-LNWR 2-2-2 *Cornwall*, which was stored at Crewe works, which had been the mainstay of the LNWR. (HMRS)

◄◄ A former Midland Railway 4-4-0 picking up water, while other troughs can be seen nearer the camera. (HMRS)

◄ The LMS inherited four London termini, including Euston and St Pancras. This is the grand frontage afforded St Pancras by the Midland Hotel, 1920s. (HMRS)

Did you know?

The broad spread of the LMS network was largely due to the Midland Railway, which had bought the Belfast & Northern Counties Railway in Northern Ireland and renamed it the Northern Counties Committee; had bought the London, Tilbury & Southern Railway; and had become a partner with the London & South Western Railway (post-Grouping, this became the Southern Railway) on the Somerset & Dorset Railway, as well as penetrating East Anglia with the Midland & Great Northern Joint Railway in partnership with the Great Northern Railway (post-Grouping, the LNER).

The Irish companies were not mentioned in the legislation, nor were they covered by it, as it was confined to Great Britain, but the LMS included the Northern Counties Committee, with its main line from Belfast to Londonderry and Larne, as well as a number of important branches, and the Dundalk, Newry & Greenore Railway, which it left to be managed by the Great Northern Railway of Ireland (GNR(I)).

Many of the companies absorbed into the LMS were substantial ventures in themselves. No less than four of them had London termini, including the former London & North Western terminus at Euston, the Midland at St Pancras and the North London at Broad Street; the London, Tilbury & Southend had the smallest of all the London termini at Fenchurch Street. The first two of these railways were substantial and post-Grouping their managements were eager to come out on top; the Lancashire & Yorkshire, despite merging with the LNWR on the eve of Grouping, had its own ideas. North of the border, there was rivalry between the Glasgow & South Western and the Caledonian.

The LMS competed with the LNER between London and Southend, and also between the former city and Scotland, with both companies serving the main Scottish cities. As well, it competed with the LNER on routes such as those from London to Manchester, and with the GWR between London and Birmingham, as well as to Merseyside, with the addition of the steam packet services to the Irish Republic as well. It faced competition to Northern Ireland from the Belfast Steamship Company and Burns & Laird.

It also competed with itself, serving Edinburgh, Glasgow and Aberdeen from both Euston and St Pancras.

Like the other members of the Big Four, the LMS operated ports, shipping and hotels, owning Europe's largest chain. It was the world's largest railway owner of hotels and the largest railway operator of ships. It was a major owner of inland waterways with more than 540 miles of canals, of which 490 miles were in England.

In 1938 the LMS operated 6,870 route miles of railway on the mainland of Great Britain alone. Its ferry services from Heysham and Stranraer to Northern Ireland, and from Holyhead to Dublin, were successful. Nevertheless, despite the progress made between Grouping and the outbreak of the Second World War, the LMS struggled to make a profit and dividends were scarce.

Although a whole year had been set aside to create a management and organisational structure that would make the new grouped company work, organising such a disparate and widespread set of railway companies into a cohesive whole was a massive problem. Unification was not helped by the struggles for dominance between the senior managers of the former Midland Railway (MR) and their counterparts in the LNWR; while in Scotland, the Caledonian Railway (CR) established itself as the dominant force and policy setter.

There was also infighting between the two major locomotive works at Crewe, ex-LNWR, and Derby, ex-MR. The MR was famous for its policy of small locomotives, and this contributed to the LMS having the lowest main-line speeds of any of the Big Four, although the earlier belief held by the LNWR that 45mph was good enough

didn't help. On the plus side, the LNWR had begun electrification of its London suburban network, while the MR's policy of centralised train control was adopted and

Did you know?

While the rivalries in England were between the former LNWR and the Midland Railway, in Scotland they were between the Caledonian Railway and the Glasgow & South Western Railway (GSWR). Despite the CR being the dominant railway in Scotland, whenever rationalisation was made, it was usually the GSWR way that was chosen. In England it was the Midland Railway port for the Irish Sea traffic that was chosen.

➤ The LMS inherited the North London Railway's electrified line from Euston to Watford, seen here, which had passed into LNWR ownership. (HMRS)

proved successful. Both the LNWR and MR had a reputation for comfortable main-line rolling stock.

The LMS constantly looked across the Atlantic to the United States for inspiration, although it rejected a forward-looking suggestion from ICI, a major freight customer, that it should drop wagon-load freight and concentrate on train-load freight between major centres. One director, or in LMS terms 'vice president', once admitted that the LMS may have been too big to be managed efficiently. It standardised the production of rolling stock and experimented with diesel traction, but only in its marshalling yards did it do this wholeheartedly.

The first step towards organising the LMS into a single, united company came with the creation of operating divisions. The president, Sir Josiah (later Lord) Stamp, was appointed in 1926, and in 1931 there

◄◄ Sir William Stanier was headhunted from GWR by Sir Josiah Stamp. He introduced many GWR design features and was responsible for the company's two outstanding series of Pacific express locomotives. (Royal Society for the Arts & Sciences)

◄ An ex-Midland Railway 4-4-0, which was typical of the everyday traction available to the LMS post-Grouping. (HMRS)

was a new chief mechanical engineer, Sir William Stanier, recruited from the GWR. From this time a more cohesive strategy was adopted and the public began to notice the new company. Costs were analysed and working practices standardised, and

◀◀ The works train used for maintaining the line was usually relegated to the oldest freight locomotives, such as this veteran 0-6-0. (HMRS)

◀ A train approaching workers on the line would proceed with caution, and a temporary permanent way slack would be set in place. (HMRS)

as funds permitted, this soon extended to new equipment.

At Derby, a research laboratory and testing facility was opened, and in 1938 this was joined by the world's first School of Transport.

The Midland policy of small locomotives led to much double-heading, which meant

double the number of drivers and firemen on each train. Not for nothing did one railway author, when compiling a *Railway Alphabet* for younger readers, write:

M is for Midland with engines galore
With two to each train and asking
for more!

It took some time to overcome the legacy of small locomotives, but a policy of scrap and build saw a steady supply of new locomotives, carriages and goods wagons. However, the company failed to introduce large 40-ton mineral wagons other than to supply the company's own power station.

None of the grouped companies set about rationalising their networks and administration with the enthusiasm expected by the politicians and their advisers. As such, line closures were fewer than was anticipated.

Sir Guy Granet, a barrister, was general manager of the Midland Railway from 1906. He received a knighthood in 1911. On Grouping, he became the LMS's first deputy chairman and then chairman in 1924. Over the next three years, almost single-handedly, he introduced the LMS to an American management style, even adopting titles such as 'president' and 'vice president'. He retired in 1927 and was replaced by Sir Josiah Stamp, who became the company's president.

Stamp created a four-man executive, later increased to seven, which fulfilled the role of general manager and an officers' committee. Stamp came from outside the industry and his management practices, like those of Granet, were those currently in vogue in the United States; for example, work study. In June 1938 he was elevated to the peerage, becoming Baron Stamp of Shortlands. In 1941, when Stamp was negotiating with the government over terms for the state control of railways during the Second World War, he was killed in an air raid along with his wife and eldest son.

Sir Henry Fowler of the MR became the first chief mechanical engineer (CME) and was ordered to produce more powerful

▼ For most of the first ten years, Sir Henry Fowler, formerly of the Midland, was the chief mechanical engineer. The Midland didn't only have express engines; this was Fowler's 0-6-0T tank engine, usually known as a 'Jinty'. (HMRS)

➤ Sir Guy Granet became chairman of the LMS in 1924 and was one of those who espoused American management practices. (*LMS Magazine*)

➤➤ Sir Josiah Stamp succeeded Granet. He became a prominent figure in the industry, becoming chairman of the Railway Companies Association. (*LMS Magazine*)

steam locomotives to end double-heading. This was a tall order for a CME accustomed to building small locomotives and the result was the Royal Scot 4-6-0, which still fell short of what was needed. He retired in 1930 and was briefly replaced by Sir Ernest Lemon, who was soon promoted to Vice President Railway Traffic, Operating & Commercial, where he was responsible for the modernisation of the LMS motive power depots.

In 1931 Fowler's true successor, Sir William Stanier, was recruited from the GWR. One of his first achievements was to end the Crewe/Derby battles. He also started a massive locomotive rationalisation and building programme that saw the number of classes fall from 404 in 1932 to 132 by 1938, while the number of locomotives needed to operate the system fell by 26 per cent.

◄ Sir Henry Fowler struggled to create harmony between the inherited locomotive and carriages works, but he was also responsible for the LMS's growing interest in diesel shunters. (Institution of Electrical Engineers)

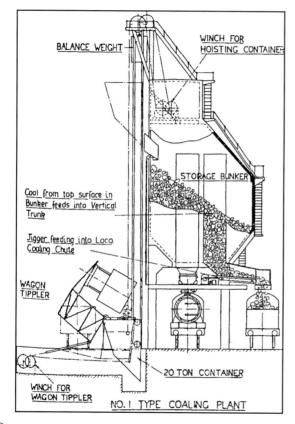

BALANCE WEIGHT

WINCH FOR HOISTING CONTAINER

STORAGE BUNKER

Coal from top surface in Bunker feeds into Vertical Trunk

Jigger feeding into Loco. Cooling Chute

WAGON TIPPLER

20 TON CONTAINER

WINCH FOR WAGON TIPPLER

NO. 1 TYPE COALING PLANT

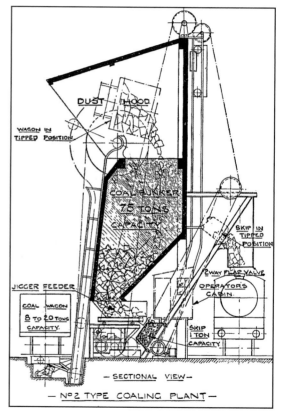

DUST HOOD

WAGON IN TIPPED POSITION

COAL BUNKER 75 TONS CAPACITY

SKIP IN TIPPED POSITION

2 WAY FLAP VALVE

OPERATOR'S CABIN

JIGGER FEEDER

COAL WAGON 8 TO 20 TONS CAPACITY.

SKIP 1 TON CAPACITY

— SECTIONAL VIEW —

— Nº2 TYPE COALING PLANT —

28

Stanier was Swindon-trained, but he showed he was not opposed to the belief that only a Pacific could provide the power needed and immediately set about creating a locomotive with a 4-6-2 wheel arrangement. The result was the *Princess Royal*, and she appeared in 1933 as the first of a class of powerful new locomotives. Next came the new 4-6-0 mixed traffic locomotive in 1934, the famous Black 5, owing much to the GWR's Hall class, while the year after came the third engine, the 2-8-0 heavy freight locomotive. The last two locomotives were effectively mass-produced, with 842 4-6-0s and 852 2-8-0s. Stanier's designs were to become locomotive classics, but they had a low level of superheating, a GWR failing which Stanier eventually put right.

Stanier's deputy as CME from 1937 was Charles Fairbairn, who had studied under Henry Fowler at the Midland Railway's Derby works from 1910 to 1912; he had then joined Siemens, where he worked on the electrification of the North Eastern Railway's Newport–Shildon freight line. Fairbairn joined the LMS in 1934 as chief

Did you know?

When Lord Stamp was killed in an air raid in 1941, his wife and eldest son and heir were also victims. The Inland Revenue did not miss the opportunity to ensure that death duties were levied not just on Lord Stamp's estate, but also on that of his elder son; therefore, the younger son who inherited had to pay double death duties.

◀◀ A 'No. 1' coaling plant, which uses a bucket lift system to take coal from the wagons 'tippled' to fill the coal hopper. (*LMS Magazine*)

◀ The 'No. 2', by contrast, lifted the coal to replenish the hopper. Instead of a gang of men labouring on a coaling stage, these plants could be worked by one man, often the locomotive fireman. (*LMS Magazine*)

electrical engineer before finally becoming chief mechanical engineer in 1944; the following year, however, he died suddenly. His achievements at the LMS included the large-scale introduction of diesel-electric shunting locomotives.

Stanier was responsible for modernising many other aspects of operation, such as the coaling of locomotives. This was a time-consuming and filthy operation when carried out manually, but massive concrete, mechanised coaling towers were built that could empty a coal wagon and tip the contents into a bunker ready for loading into locomotive tenders, with the operation triggered by the driver or fireman. The small bunkers on tank engines could not use this form of coaling.

Belfast-born Sir William Wood joined the LMS from the Northern Counties Committee in 1924 after a brief spell as the first financial director of the Ministry of Transport, formed in 1919. Initially, he was assistant to the accountant general, becoming controller of costs and statistics in 1927, and in 1930 he was elevated to the much superior position of vice president of the executive committee. Wood was knighted in 1937. When Stamp was killed, Wood took over as the company's president and also became a member of the Railway Executive Committee. Post-nationalisation, he spent five years as a member of the British Transport Commission, the irony of which was that he had previously believed the LMS to be too big to be managed efficiently.

◄ A Princess Royal locomotive hauls an express bound for Scotland past sidings and industrial premises – the popular view of the LMS. (HMRS)

While the early years after the Grouping of 1923 had seen a lack of direction and indecision, as well as a Midland-oriented approach, Stanier insisted on design guidelines based on GWR practice for locomotives. He introduced handsome tapered boilers and Belpaire fireboxes, Swindon-style axleboxes with large axle journals, and cylinders with large valves; the drivers and firemen were not forgotten either, with better grouping of controls in a comfortable cab. He also adopted Walschaerts valve gear, invented and named after a Belgian engineer, mounted on the outside of locomotives for ease of maintenance. The main LMS-era steam locomotives catered for express, mixed traffic, capable of handling passenger or fast goods trains, and goods trains.

Before Stanier's arrival, Fowler introduced the Royal Scot-class 4-6-0, not to be confused with the train of the same name. These locomotives first appeared in 1927 and were seen on some of the longest through workings, such as the one between Euston and Carlisle, which was 299 miles, and Crewe and Perth, 291 miles with the ascents of both Shap and Beattock; trains

▼ For Fowler, a 4-6-0 express locomotive was adequate. This is one of his Patriot class, seen after nationalisation. (HMRS)

of as much as 440 tons were hauled at an average speed of 52mph. Later, these were modified with Stanier-style tapered boilers and improved cylinders and piston valves. In this form, after nationalisation during the 1948 Locomotive Interchange Trials, they were pitted against Pacific 4-6-2 locomotives.

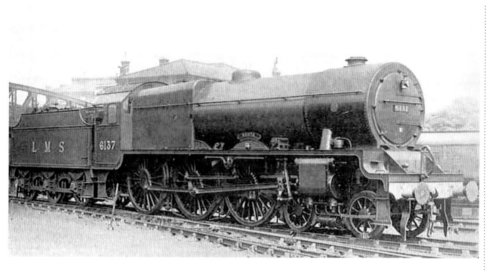

◄◄ The Mid-Day Scot streaks through Stafford in March 1938 headed by 4-6-0 Royal Scot No. 6103 *Royal Scots Fusilier*. (HMRS)

◄ Another Royal Scot, No. 6137 *Vesta*, but without the usual smoke deflectors on either side of the smokebox. (HMRS)

A development of the LNWR Claughton-class 4-6-0 locomotives was the Jubilee class. While the original idea was to give the Claughton class larger boilers, Stanier used an enlarged Claughton boiler combined with many features of the Royal Scots to provide a useful locomotive class that was nicknamed the 'Baby Scots'; the modified Claughtons were known officially, however, as the Patriot class.

Also pre-dating Stanier was a 2-6-4 passenger tank locomotive for commuter services and busier branch lines, and the first of these, introduced in 1927, had MR pattern

➤ The LMS was sufficiently proud of its track maintenance that it commissioned a poster showing men working on the line, using the leading artists of the day. (LMS)

➤➤ An ex-sleeping car that has been converted to provide sleeping and mess accommodation for track workers maintaining the line. (HMRS)

LMS THE PERMANENT WAY
RELAYING
BY STANHOPE FORBES, R.A.

The inside of the mess room aboard one of the accommodation carriages. The men shared the cooking and other chores among themselves. It seems untidy, but suspiciously clean! (HMRS)

A breakdown train with its locomotive at the ready. Breakdown trains were sometimes used by civil engineers when heavy lifting was needed, such as in the rebuilding of a bridge. (HMRS)

boilers and outside Walschaerts valve gear. Later versions had a tapered Stanier-style boiler which was more expensive to build but had lower maintenance costs. Most were two-cylinder locomotives, but a more powerful three-cylinder design was built for services to Southend; the town was promised, but denied, electrification.

By adapting existing designs for many locomotive classes, Stanier could turn his

▲ No. 6100 was the first of the Royal Scot class. She is seen here at Llangollen, beautifully preserved and in steam, but without smoke deflectors. (Das48)

passenger services needed a Pacific locomotive; that is, one with a 4-6-2 wheel arrangement. The company's first Pacifics were the Princess Royal class, with the first two completed in 1933. Later versions, built from 1935 onwards, had a higher level of superheating. Although eclipsed by the Duchess class that followed, these locomotives were capable of outstanding performance and were certainly a step in the right direction. This was proved when one of the Princess Royal class, *Princess Elizabeth*, showed that Stanier was right and earned the LMS its first speed record.

attention to much-needed new classes. A powerful express locomotive was required for the demanding West Coast route, with the weight to be drawn increased to 500 tons without assistance; there was also a desperate need for a new heavy freight locomotive and for a mixed traffic 4-6-0 locomotive.

Nevertheless, the long distances and the heavy loads typical of so many LMS

The most famous of Stanier's designs – and had it not been for the Second World War it would have been the most numerous – was the Class 5 4-6-0 mixed traffic locomotive, more commonly known as the Black 5. It had many GWR features, including a tapered boiler, but differed in having outside Walschaerts valve gear.

Following the Black 5s were the 8F-class 2-8-0 freight engines, with a general appearance similar to the Black 5, but with a smaller boiler. In 1939 this was chosen as the wartime standard locomotive for Britain's railways and the government ordered large numbers for use in the UK and overseas, where many remained after the war. This was the most numerous Stanier design.

Finally, there was the Duchess class, of which the early examples had streamlined exteriors and were introduced in 1937 for the Coronation Scot express, with non-streamlined versions introduced from 1938 onwards. The first locomotive, No. 6220 *Coronation*, set a record of 114mph on a special run.

The removal of the Railway Passenger Duty in 1929 (on condition that the sums saved by the railway companies were used for new investment to help reduce unemployment) and the availability of low-interest loans backed by the Treasury in the years that followed saw the LMS do its best to modernise. In 1934 new rolling stock included 232 steam locomotives, 159 new boilers for the rebuilding of older

▼ The Jubilee-class locomotives were the ultimate 4-6-0s for express passenger working. This is No. 5690 *Leander* at Castleton, where she is working on the Keighley & Worth Valley Railway. (David Ingham)

42

Did you know?

The former LNWR and Midland steam locomotives had regulators that worked in opposite directions. The Midland practice was the standard for most railways, and when an ex-Midland driver found himself in a former LNWR steam locomotive cab, he had to remember that the regulator worked the other way. Many forgot, and locomotives ended up being reversed through the shed wall of a roundhouse or into the turntable well, putting the shed out of action for several hours.

►► This is the record-breaking *Princess Royal* undergoing a major examination at the Crewe locomotive works. (HMRS)

◄ *Coronation* achieved the British speed record of 114mph in June 1937. The achievement was afforded front-page treatment, as this *Daily Sketch* page shows. (*Daily Sketch*)

➤ *Fury*, the trials locomotive for high-pressure steam, was withdrawn after a fatal accident when a steam pipe burst. (HMRS)

➤➤ In the hunt for extra power one of the Princess class, nicknamed the 'Turbomotive', was completed as a turbine steam locomotive, but no more were built after that. She survived into nationalisation but was scrapped after an accident shortly afterwards. (HMRS)

locomotives, 674 new carriages and 5,365 new wagons.

There was also the opportunity to experiment. The belief that higher boiler pressures would help the steam locomotive to a bright future resulted in an experimental steam locomotive, *Fury*, with a high-pressure, three-stage Schmidt-Henschel boiler. She was very disappointing and after a serious accident she was withdrawn.

One Princess Royal Pacific was built as a geared turbine locomotive, which became known throughout the company as the 'Turbomotive'. The logic was impeccable: geared turbines had displaced pistons to enhance the speed of steamers at sea, so why not on the rails as well? Unfortunately, the experiment was not a success, and although the Turbomotive ran for 450,000 miles and remained in service until 1950, she was a liability and spent long periods in the workshops with lubrication problems and gear train failures.

Successful though they were, the Princess Royal class was soon overtaken by the steady rise in train weights, meaning that something still more powerful was needed. Streamlining was next, with the Duchess or Coronation Pacifics, the first ten of which were streamlined, although those with the streamlined casing had it removed in the immediate post-war period.

The importance of streamlining was not purely aesthetic. The shape of a conventional steam locomotive was scarcely aerodynamic, and the railway locomotive designers were already as aware as any aeroplane designer of the impact on performance of what the latter would refer to as 'drag'. It was also well known that high winds could affect performance. The LMS Research Centre at Derby included a wind tunnel, albeit only large enough to test models, but the Coronation design was tested in this wind tunnel, with artificial winds and gales blasted at the model head-on from the front, sideways and at various different angles across the track.

Given the largest boiler and firebox that the loading gauge would allow, with a grate area 11 per cent larger than on the Princess Royals, and with the inside valve gears removed, the Duchess was the most powerful steam locomotive ever to run in the British Isles. This combination of steam locomotives gave the LMS what it needed, especially once the Royal Scots were rebuilt.

➤ Typical of the rolling stock used on suburban trains is this rake of carriages seen in a siding. These are the older six-wheelers, which would have been uncomfortable compared with later bogie carriages. (HMRS)

Despite its admiration for much that was American, the LMS maintained that many of its passengers preferred to have the privacy of a compartment rather than an open saloon. Both types were built, however, for both first- and third-class passengers, although on many trains the open saloons were marshalled next to the kitchen cars to allow them to be used as dining cars.

The first step forward was to standardise the dimensions of new rolling stock, with the LMS opting for 57ft in length and 9ft in width, the dimensions favoured by the LNWR and, latterly, by the Midland. Despite this move and the centralisation of LMS decision-making, the standard was not set rigidly, and the company produced a few 54ft-long carriages when this was deemed necessary, and even some 51ft carriages for Glasgow's Cathcart Circle line.

At Derby and Wolverhampton carriage parts were prefabricated to speed up production, so the main production line was engaged in final assembly only and the more detailed work was handled away from it. 'All-steel' carriages, except for the roofs and window frames which were still made of wood, were the next step, easing mass production, but also, from 1929 onwards, it reduced the demand for mainly imported timber and provided work for the steel industry, which was badly affected by the Depression years.

Considerable orders for new carriages were placed outside the company with independent carriage builders as the company's own works could not keep pace with the demand. As a sop to conservatism, the new all-steel carriages were still lined out, even to the extent that panels, which no longer existed, were picked out, making

➤ The somewhat spartan interior of one of the North London electric sets. Later LMS-built steam-hauled suburban stock would have been more comfortable, but no doubt less clean. (HMRS)

➤➤ The change from six- or eight-wheel stock to bogie stock meant disposing of redundant carriages. Some large passenger carriages were converted into 'camping carriages', although this one is marked 'caravan'. (HMRS)

◀◀ A small 0-4-4T tank engine takes a suburban train out of Glasgow Queen Street. The carriages are much younger than the locomotive. (HMRS)

◀ The LMS bought a small number of Garratt 2-6-0 + 0-6-2 articulated steam locomotives from Beyer-Peacock, but these did not achieve their full potential due to influence from the Midland engineers at Derby. (Colour-Rail)

painting an expensive business. By this time the LMS was building only carriages with end doors for its longer-distance services.

'All-steel' was an apt description, but the interiors were trimmed with wood and in later years the LMS had a small notice advising passengers of the type of wood used and its place of origin, which was always within the British Empire. Seats on the new carriages were padded and

Did you know?

Ever wanted to be able to choose your fellow passengers? The LMS ran 'club trains' from the Fylde Coast and from North Wales to Manchester. These had a first-class carriage reserved for people who had to be voted on as members by their fellow passengers, making it a club. There were strict rules and an attendant served tea. Later, a third-class carriage was allocated. To this day, commuter trains on these routes are still known as 'club trains'.

sprung. The new first-class compartments had just four seats so that everyone had the prized corner seat, but the first-class open carriages had one and two abreast seating, as one would find today. In 1930 windows were made deeper, while the overall carriage length was stretched to 60ft, not to increase capacity but to

SNOWDONIA
LONDON MIDLAND AND SCOTTISH RAILWAY

◄◄ Doors to every compartment and even carriages without corridors were still built for suburban- and branch-line use, as this picture of a 2-6-4T with a suburban train leaving Glasgow Central shows. (HMRS)

◄ While the LMS used advertising to show its pride in its operations, it also took a hard-headed commercial approach to marketing services to holiday destinations, including Snowdonia in North Wales. (NRM/ Science Museum Photograph)

The Lake District was a popular holiday destination firmly within LMS territory, with much of the area covered by the old Furness Railway. (LMS)

This dramatic locomotive footplate setting is for the Night Mail, which was an informal name for a fast mail train; it sometimes consisted entirely of travelling Post Office cars, but at other times included passenger carriages as well. (LMS)

SCOT PASSES SCOT

By Bryan de Grineau.

LMS 10·0 A.M. EUSTON TO GLASGOW AND EDINBURGH
10·0 A.M. GLASGOW AND EDINBURGH TO EUSTON

◄ 'Scot passes Scot' emphasised not just the speed of the prestigious service, but also its daily frequency. This was the way to travel, especially if time was of the essence. (LMS)

improve comfort: third-class compartments went from 6ft between partitions to 6ft 6in, while first-class compartments went up to 7ft 6in. The improvement was temporary, and clearly too expensive at a time of financial hardship, so carriage lengths soon reverted back to 57ft, and the third-class compartment was reduced to 6ft 3in – a compromise. This amount of room was also provided on suburban trains.

In contrast to his work on locomotives, Stanier did not bring GWR ideas with him for carriages, which would have been a backward step. The next step was for window frames and roofs to be made of steel also, and for window frames to be rounded and sliding window ventilators placed in the upper part of the main window for the first time. Comfort for the third-class passenger on the main-line expresses was improved when compartment carriages had their accommodation reduced from eight seats to six, with armrests and reading lights, so they almost rivalled first class on some companies.

Carriages became completely flush-sided, enhancing the 'modern' look and no doubt helping to reduce drag. At first, the lining tried to convince the casual observer that this was still a traditional carriage, but by the mid-1930s this was simplified, with plain lines above and below the windows and below the roof, while in some carriages for more humble trains, gold paint was replaced by deep yellow.

Until 1928 sleeping cars were only available to first-class passengers. That year, the LMS, GWR and LNER introduced third-class sleeping cars, which accommodated four passengers to a compartment. In reality, they were more akin to the couchettes found on continental railways as the compartments could be converted back to day use, at which point they could seat eight passengers. They lacked the amenities, such as a hand wash basin, that first-class passengers were accustomed to. By the mid-1930s, purpose-built third-class sleeping cars were introduced with permanent berths, but still four to a compartment.

The LMS did not ignore articulation, but did not pursue it with the enthusiasm of the LNER. As well as the articulated carriages built for the Coronation Scot, pairs of articulated carriages were built for excursion trains. Some three-carriage sets were built for suburban use, as well as a prototype diesel multiple unit of futuristic streamlined design, to be mentioned in the next chapter.

During the 1920s and 1930s there was some rationalisation of freight handling and management so that by 1938, the company's freight business was generally profitable. This was largely because the LMS, LNER and GWR standardised and co-ordinated their freight sales forces, or canvassers, and outside London combined

➤ The 0-8-0 was often used to move heavy coal trains. On congested parts of the line it had to give way to passenger trains, and a driver and fireman could spend their whole shift on a locomotive without moving. (HMRS)

➤➤ Even tank locomotives could handle heavy freight, such as this 0-8-4T. The size of the bunker suggests that it was not simply a yard shunter. (HMRS)

their freight collection and delivery services. Nevertheless, all the railway companies were hampered by what was known as the 'common carrier obligation', which meant they had to accept whatever traffic was offered, profitable or not. Freight rates

LMS   **A MIDLAND COALFIELD**
BY
NORMAN WILKINSON, R.I.

◄◄ The LMS was keen to use containers to reduce transhipment costs, time and the risk of damage or pilferage when consignments were transferred between road and rail, as can be seen in this view of a goods train. (HMRS)

◄ This poster of a Midland coalfield hints at the importance of the LMS to industry, and perhaps also of the importance of coal to the railways, both as a fuel and as the main form of freight traffic. (NRM/Science Museum Photograph)

➤ The mixed goods train was a feature of all the railways. Often, the locomotive would be uncoupled to shunt wagons into sidings, but this 2-8-0 Stanier 8F goods locomotive would have been reserved for faster through goods trains. (HMRS)

➤➤ Another Stanier 8F 2-8-0; it is between duties and sitting in a yard. Locomotives like this accelerated freight services and provided the power that was needed. (HMRS)

for most items were controlled by the government.

With the exception of the Southern, and to some extent the Great Western, the railway companies were heavily dependent on freight traffic as opposed to the more glamorous passenger business. Coal was a major traffic as it was used for heating and

power, in the home as well as in the office; it was also used, of course, by the railways themselves. Every small station had a goods yard, which would be home to at least one coal merchant.

Resistance by the mine owners to larger coal wagons capable of carrying 20 tons or more meant that productivity improvements were difficult; the typical coal train, therefore, ran at between 5 and 10mph and consisted of wagons filled with 5 tons of coal. These trains had a low priority and had to move into sidings to allow passenger expresses to pass.

The railways were suffering from competition from road transport, invigorated after the First World War by the release into civilian life of men who had been taught to drive and trained to maintain road vehicles. At the same time, the War Office was selling off surplus army vehicles at bargain prices. Yet the need to

◄◄ An 0-8-0 sits idly in a yard, with a water tower in the background and, just to the side of it, what may be a coaling plant. (HMRS)

◄ A coaling plant at work, with several tons of coal being dropped into the locomotive tender within minutes. For an express locomotive, 4 or 5 tons was not unusual and for the large Pacifics it could be more. (HMRS)

maintain freight services (the term used by most of the railways rather than 'goods') was such that the 'pick-up freight' was a common sight. This was a goods train that had to call at every goods yard to drop off or pick up wagons, and if the yard was too small to sustain a shunting engine, the train's locomotive had to be detached to handle this function, although in some small yards a heavy horse would be used for shunting wagons.

Wagon-load freight did exist, as did train-load freight, especially to power stations and gasworks, but much of the traffic consisted of smaller items, so the goods yard would have a staff to receive and deliver consignments, no matter how small or large. The LMS set targets, or quotas, for freight traffic and awarded prizes for good performance. One stationmaster from a small country station, on having a large contract from a major customer suddenly land on his station, was surprised to be summoned to head office at Euston and be given an award.

Did you know?

Many associated the term 'freight' with American English and 'goods' as standard or Oxford English. In fact, most of the railway companies used the term 'freight' rather than 'goods'. Salesmen, known as canvassers, were employed to call on freight customers. The canvassers were expected to be knowledgeable about passenger services as well, and could sometimes provide first-class tickets as inducements for business given.

Although the LMS inherited the LNWR's electrification of the North London Railway (NLR), and also the Lancashire & Yorkshire Railway's Lancaster–Morecambe–Heysham scheme, both had been in response to competition from electric street tramways, and the company was so convinced that the future lay in steam that its main focus was on improving the steam locomotive. The LNWR/NLR system was extended to Rickmansworth; the only two electrification schemes actually carried out by the LMS were the Manchester South Junction & Altrincham (MSJ&A), operated jointly with the LNER, and the Wirral Lines. The 8-mile long MSJ&A was completed in 1931 and used 1,500V DC overhead collection, but for the Wirral Lines, completed in 1938, 650V DC was used with a third rail to ensure efficient through working with the Mersey Railway.

LMS trains could operate on either third or third and fourth rail systems, so the system used not one, two or even three methods of electrification, but four.

▼ Clearly taken shortly after Grouping, as this ex-Midland 0-6-0 still has its numbered tender, this is a train of vans, and most probably a special. (HMRS)

◄◄ The other form of electrification inherited was the small fleet of battery-electric shunters from the Lancashire & Yorkshire Railway. (HMRS)

◄ The first LMS diesel shunter was in fact a rebuild of a standard 0-6-0T tank engine, with a driving cab at each end, but it clearly worked well for the LMS to continue to develop the concept. (HMRS)

The main emphasis was on shunting, with the LMS inheriting battery-electric shunters which had long lives. Also, from 1932 the LMS started to experiment with diesel-powered shunters, although the first was a converted 0-6-0 tank locomotive.

74

◄◄ The Vulcan Foundry provided the LMS with its next diesel shunter, with a cab in the middle and a 275hp engine. (HMRS)

◄ Armstrong Whitworth built a prototype 250hp diesel shunter which looked more like the shunter we know today, followed by more powerful 300hp shunters. These engines carried sufficient fuel for a week's work. Twenty of the type shown were ordered. (HMRS)

◄◄ The LMS built and conducted trials with this futuristic, articulated, three-car diesel-hydraulic multiple unit. It was painted bright Post Office red to waist level and silver above. Trials proved successful, with speeds of almost 80mph achieved. (HMRS)

◄ The LMS ordered two 1,600hp diesel-electric locomotives for main-line trials, but only the first of these, numbered 10000, was ready before nationalisation and was painted black. It had cabs at each end and was intended to operate in tandem with a single driver. (Colour-Rail)

➤ The two electrification schemes undertaken by the LMS included the Wirral Lines, which were electrified on the third-rail system to ensure through working with the Mersey Railway. (HMRS)

Did you know?

The main reason for the reluctance of many railway engineers to advocate greater use of the diesel and electric train was that steam was still seen as the advanced technology of the day; journals even carried learned papers on the great potential that still existed for the steam locomotive. In fact, on express trains steam remained faster than electric or diesel, until the Germans introduced the record-breaking 'Flying Hamburger' express diesel between Berlin and Hamburg.

After initial setbacks, due to this and other new diesel shunters being underpowered, large orders for reliable diesel shunters appeared, and more than seventy were in service by nationalisation.

Perhaps the real 'what might have been' lay in the three diesel-electric locomotives that were ordered during 1946–47. Two were built at Derby and of Co-Co, that is with each bogie having three powered axles and no unpowered axles, and configuration with 1,600hp English Electric diesel engines; while the third was a Bo-Bo, that is with each bogie having two powered axles and no unpowered axles, built by the North British Locomotive Company using an 800hp Paxman diesel and intended for secondary main lines and cross-country services. Only the first of the two main-line locomotives, No. 10000, was completed just before nationalisation,

so she appeared with the raised letters LMS on her side casing.

There was also a three-car diesel unit with articulated carriages and futuristic bow-ended driving cabs built by Stanier at Derby. Using diesel hydraulic traction and six Leyland diesel engines, two to a carriage, the train was designed to operate on secondary main lines at 75mph, but on trials almost 80mph was reached.

There was an air of romance and adventure about a long-distance journey by railway, something which the Big Four railway companies did much to foster as they sought to increase passenger traffic between the wars. An obstacle at the beginning was that on the main routes between London and Scotland, in the wake of the railway races of 1888 and 1895, the LMS and LNER were hindered by an agreement that the day expresses would run to Glasgow and Edinburgh in eight and a half hours.

Journey times started to be reduced with major accelerations in 1932, but it was in 1936 that the LNER forced the LMS into action by announcing that it would celebrate the coronation of King George VI the following year with a streamlined express running between London and Edinburgh. It took just weeks for the LMS to put one of its new but unstreamlined Pacifics, *Princess Elizabeth*, on a high-speed run from London Euston to Glasgow Central with a rake of seven carriages, far less than the locomotive would normally have handled. On 16 November 1936 *Princess Elizabeth* completed the journey of 401.4 miles in just five hours, fifty-three and a half minutes. On the return run, despite having eight carriages in high winds and heavy rain, she took just five hours, forty-four and a quarter minutes, giving an average speed of 70mph throughout the journey.

The main LMS expresses included the following.

The **Royal Scot**, which was first named in 1927 when the train was limited to through passengers from Euston to Edinburgh and Glasgow only, albeit with a stop at Carnforth for examination and a locomotive change before two 4-4-0 compounds took

◄ Although the only speed record claimed by the LMS was for a Coronation-class locomotive, the company's first Pacific locomotives were of the Princess Royal class, which gave the LMS the high-powered locomotives it needed for handling heavy trains and the long, steep gradients at Shap and Beattock on the West Coast route. This is *Princess Elizabeth*. (HMRS)

➤ *Princess Elizabeth* has been beautifully preserved as a representative of the Princess Royal class and made a guest appearance at the 2012 Diamond Jubilee celebrations for HM Queen Elizabeth II. Here she is seen with BR Mk.1 carriages. (David Ingham)

over for the summits of Shap and Beattock. The Edinburgh and Glasgow portions were parted at Symington. Eventually both sections ran separately, non-stop, from Euston to Edinburgh and Glasgow during the busy summer months. The journey time was steadily reduced from 1932 onwards. By 1939, the journey time between Euston and Glasgow was just seven hours.

The **Coronation Scot**, which vied with the Royal Scot as the most famous of the LMS expresses, was in many ways the LMS's answer to the LNER's rival, named

◀ The LMS set about building the most powerful steam locomotives of the day: the Coronation class, with their art deco styling and highly streamlined appearance. Later versions were built without the streamlining as the Duchess class. (HMRS)

▶ Royal Scot No. 6107, *Argyll & Sutherland Fusiliers*, shows even the best trains had a variety of rolling stock for many years. (HMRS)

simply the Coronation. This truly prestigious train was inaugurated to celebrate the coronation of King George VI in 1937. New streamlined steam locomotives were built, but locomotives of the same class were built in streamlined and unstreamlined forms. Initially, standard LMS carriages were used, but repainted in the blue with silver stripes of the locomotives, with the lining continued down the train. Later, these were joined by specially built carriages, which had pressure

ventilation and articulation, and in 1939 the livery of the train changed to red with gold stripes. The special carriages were sent with a locomotive to the 1939 New York World Fair and spent the war there, although the much-needed locomotive was repatriated shortly after the start of hostilities.

The **Comet** replaced an earlier up evening express running from Manchester to London Euston and was first named in 1932. It could leave Manchester London Road at 5.40 p.m., taking less than four hours to reach Euston at 9.20 p.m. It bypassed Crewe and stopped only at Stafford, with the run onwards over the 133.6 miles to London taking just 128 minutes, making it one of the fastest trains on the LMS.

The train was a heavy burden for its 4-6-0 Royal Scot locomotive with a minimum of eleven carriages, and sometimes, if extra vehicles were attached, a 4-4-0 compound was provided as a pilot. The late morning down train was not as deserving of the name Comet, being much slower.

The **Irish Mails**, a description rather than a formal name, were not a single train but usually two trains a day in each direction, and noted more for their considerable weight than for speed; even in peacetime trains of up to sixteen or seventeen carriages could be pulled along the North Wales main line between Holyhead and Chester by a single 4-6-0 Royal Scot locomotive. Pacific locomotives were used for a time during the 1930s, but the service soon reverted to the Royal Scots, possibly due to demand elsewhere for the more powerful Pacifics.

The morning departures were of day trains for which the restaurant cars were, reputedly, outstanding for their food and service. The night trains included both first- and third-class sleeping cars, but whether the extra cost of travelling in these was worth it must be questionable, as on the down journey passengers had to leave their snug berths at 2.20 a.m., when the train reached Holyhead, and walk to the waiting ferry. Far happier was the up passenger, who could be off the ferry and into his berth by midnight, and could remain in it for some time after reaching Euston. All four trains daily included two Post Office sorting cars, with their mail bag apparatus used at Nuneaton, Llandudno Junction and the Menai Bridge, before the trains crossed through the Britannia Tubular Bridge into Anglesey.

The **Midday Scot** was the successor to the West Coast companies' express Corridor, but received its official title in 1927. It was one of the first Anglo-Scottish services to enjoy an accelerated schedule, initially eight hours southbound, although northbound the train required an extra five minutes. It actually left in each direction at 1.30 p.m. rather than noon, and in May 1936 the train's departure

TAKE YOUR DOG WITH YOU BY RAIL

Return Tickets at Single Rate
(AT OWNER'S RISK)

DRINKING WATER FOR DOGS CAN BE OBTAINED FROM STATION REFRESHMENT ROOMS OR ON REQUEST TO A MEMBER OF THE STATION STAFF

G.W.R. LMS L·N·E·R S.R.

◄ A joint advertisement by the four railway companies urging people to take their dogs with them when travelling by train – with water available on request at stations. (NRM/Science Museum Photograph)

➤ An elderly travelling Post Office, in which mail was sorted and dropped or picked up without the need to stop, using special apparatus. (HMRS)

time from Euston was moved back to 2 p.m., with another express taking its post-Grouping departure at 1.30 p.m. so it could run non-stop over the 158 miles to Crewe in 163 minutes. A new stop was added at Penrith and the train continued to divide at Carlisle for Glasgow and Edinburgh, while Edinburgh and Aberdeen portions parted

LMS

ABERDEEN
BRIG O' BALGOWNIE.
BY ALGERNON TALMAGE. A.R.A.

◄ An advertisement by the railway companies for one of the locations within reach of Aberdeen, a city which enjoyed competition between the LMS and LNER. (LMS)

company at Lockerbie. The Glasgow portion arrived at Glasgow Central at 9.35 p.m., while Edinburgh Princes Street was reached at 9.55 p.m.

The **Night Limited/Night Scot** came about because the overnight trains were actually faster than the day trains, taking eight hours from Euston to Glasgow, but timings were extended to just under ten hours after the First World War. (A couple of restaurant cars were, however, inserted at Carlisle so that the Glasgow-bound traveller could have breakfast along the way. He would also have had a chance to read the morning newspapers, picked up during the stop at Symington.)

The **North Atlantic Express** had one of the most ambitious names ever coined for a train and was operated by the Northern Counties Committee (NCC) of the LMS. New 2-6-0 locomotives provided the power that an accelerated service required and

Did you know?
When the Duchess-class Pacifics were first introduced on the Coronation Scot express in 1937, locomotives and carriages were painted in pale blue with silver stripes that extended from the locomotive along the carriage sides. This was a break with the LMS corporate identity of red for passenger carriages and passenger express locomotives – a strange decision by a company that looked across the Atlantic for most of its management practices.

the North Atlantic Express was introduced between Belfast and the resort of Portrush, on the north coast of County Antrim. To match the new locomotives, the LMS built three new carriages with the first picture windows on NCC rolling stock and one of the coaches being completed as a buffet car. A year after its introduction, two additional carriages were built.

The new service was launched on 1 June 1934 and at first covered the 65¼-mile run in eighty minutes, with a stop of just one minute at Ballymena; in the years that followed timings were tightened, so that by 1938 the service took just seventy-three minutes, despite half the route being on a single-track railway. Between Ballymena and Belfast the service met the 'mile a minute' standard, with the 31 miles covered in thirty-one minutes.

The **Pines Express** originated in 1910 and ran between Manchester and Bournemouth, which coincidentally gave the fastest journey between the two cities, running over LNWR lines, before switching to the Midland Railway at Birmingham New Street and using Midland track for the onward journey to Bath; there, the Somerset & Dorset Joint Railway (SDJR), a joint venture between the Midland and the London & South Western Railway (LSWR), took over, although the final stretch of 7¾ miles from Broadstone through Poole to Bournemouth was on LSWR track. It was not until 1927 that the LMS named it the Pines Express, a reflection of the fact that Bournemouth was famed for its pines. In 1929, in an attempt to improve the operation of the SDJR and also cut costs, the SDJR no longer provided locomotives and these became the responsibility of the LMS, allowing the works at Highbridge to be closed, while the Southern took responsibility for the track.

In 1939 the southbound train, complete with restaurant car, left Manchester London Road at 10.10 a.m. and arrived at Bournemouth at 4.37 p.m., taking six hours, twenty-seven minutes for the 252 miles, despite 26 miles of the route being over single track. The northbound Pines Express was faster, taking six hours, sixteen minutes from Bournemouth.

There were many other expresses, including several, such as the St Mungo, the Fast Belfast and the Granite City, which ran entirely within Scotland; the Ulster Express linked first St Pancras and then Euston with Heysham for the overnight steam packet to Belfast. There were also expresses to the Lake District and the Peak District.

Although in the early days the railway companies were not allowed to operate ships, long before Grouping ferry services had become an integral part of the railway business. The LMS not only served its own shipping services, but also those of other companies, such as Burns & Laird on the services to Northern Ireland, operating from Ardrossan to Belfast; the Belfast Steamship Company's service from Liverpool to Belfast; the Isle of Man Steam Packet Company operating from Fleetwood and Liverpool; and British & Irish from Liverpool to Dublin.

The LMS had the largest steamship operation of any railway in the world, with no less than twenty-nine Irish Sea steamers with a total gross registered tonnage (grt) of 49,258; twenty-one continental steamers with a total grt of 19,917; eleven steamers on the River Clyde with a total grt of 4,523; eight river ferries with a total grt of 1,317; seventeen lake steamers with a total grt of 1,782; nine tugs, thirty-six hoppers, dredgers and barges, and seven pontoons. All this amounted to a total grt of 92,614. This may seem a small amount today, when a single cross-Channel ferry can be more than 40,000 tons, but ships were much smaller at the time and a ferry with a tonnage of around 3,000 was regarded as a substantial ship.

The company inherited the docks at Barrow from the Furness Railway, while the LNWR provided the docks at Garston, near Liverpool, and those at Deganwy Quay and Foryd Pier in Wales, as well as Holyhead on the island of Anglesey. Fleetwood had been built and operated by the LNWR and the LYR together, while the latter also had the

94

T.S.S. DUKE OF LANCASTER
LONDON MIDLAND & SCOTTISH RAILWAY
HEYSHAM & BELFAST

◄◄ The LMS inherited many ports, one of which was Grangemouth on the Forth. Here is a typical quayside scene, rail served and with loaded wagons. (HMRS)

◄ A postcard showing the *Duke of Lancaster*, one of three turbine steamers introduced by the LMS on the busy overnight ferry service between Heysham and Belfast. (LMS)

Wyre Dock and Goole on the Humber. The Midland had two docks at Bristol, Avonside and King's Wharf, plus the port of Heysham in Lancashire; on the River Thames it had a landing stage at Tilbury, the Town and West Piers at Gravesend, and docks at Poplar, where the North London Railway also had a separate facility. The Severn & Wye Joint Railway had docks on the River Severn at Lydney in Gloucestershire, while the SDJR had docks at Highbridge in Somerset.

In Scotland the Caledonian passed on its docks at Bowling, Grangemouth and Alloa, as well as the Railway Pier at Oban and piers on the Clyde at Gourock and Wemyss Bay. The Glasgow & South Western also had piers at Fairlie, Largs and Renfrew, plus docks at Ayr and Troon, all on the

FIVE ROUTES TO IRELAND.

ROYAL MAIL ROUTE.
Via HEYSHAM and BELFAST.

New Cross Channel Steamers.

"DUKE OF ARGYLL," "DUKE OF LANCASTER," "DUKE OF ROTHESAY," & "DUKE OF YORK"

will sail as follows:—

	FRIS. ONLY p.m.	SATS. ONLY p.m.	DAILY		MON. to FRI. p.m.	SATS. ONLY p.m.	SATS. ONLY. Will run from July 9th to Aug. 27th a.m.	SATS. ONLY. SUNS. p.m.
HEYSHAM dp	1050	1230	1155	BELFAST..dep	9 40	10 0	11 0	11 30 9 40
			a.m.	(Donegall Quay)	a.m.	p.m.	p.m.	p.m.
BELFAST arr. (Donegall Quay) about	5 35	7 30	6 45	HEYSHAM arr. about	4 45	4 45	7 0	6 30 4 45

Through Carriages are run between London (Euston and St. Pancras, Crewe, Leeds (Wellington), Sheffield, Halifax, Manchester (Victoria), Bolton (Trinity Street), Preston, and Heysham. Restaurant Cars are run between London (Euston), Leeds (Wellington), Bradford (Forster St.), Manchester (Victoria), and Heysham.

The Boat Train between London (Euston and St. Pancras, Birmingham (New Street), &c., and Heysham arrives and departs alongside the Steamer, therefore no expense is incurred in the transfer of Luggage.

For Reservation of Berths, write as under:—

From Heysham to Belfast:—To Marine Superintendent, HEYSHAM HARBOUR, (Telegraphic Address:—"Afloat, Liverpool") or the British and Irish Steam Railway Steamers, Heysham Harbour")

From Belfast to Heysham:—To Mr. M. SPIER, 11/13, Donegall Place, (Telegraphic Address:—"Boxline, Belfast")

Tel.: 73 & 74 (Extension 26).   Telephone: 44211.

The following charges will be made in respect of Sleeping Berths :—
Cabin de Luxe—Single, 26/3. Double, 31/6.
Saloon—Single Berth Room, 8/-; other Berths with "Made-up" Beds, 2/9 each Berth.
Steerage—Single Berth, 2/- per Berth.

Via LIVERPOOL and DUBLIN.
(British & Irish Steam Packet Co.)

	Week-days only				Week-days only	
	Mon. to Fri.	Sat. only			Mon. to Fri. from Ireland	Saturday from Ireland
LONDON (Euston)........dep	6 5 p.m.	6 8 p.m.	DUBLIN (North Wall)......dep		8 30 p.m.	11 0 p.m.
LIVERPOOL (Lime St.)........dep	9 40	9 47 p.m.	LIVERPOOL (Landing Stage) arr		6 0 a.m.	8 0 a.m.
(Landing Stage or) Princes Dock) } ..dep	10 15 p.m.	10 15 p.m.	" (Lime St.)......dep		8 15 a.m.	9 30 a.m.
DUBLIN (North Wall)............arr	6 0 a.m.	8 0 a.m.	LONDON (Euston)............arr		12 0 noon	1 45 p.m.

ROYAL MAIL ROUTE.
Via LIVERPOOL and BELFAST.
(Belfast Steamship Co.)

	Week-days only				Week-days only	
					Mon. to Fri. from Ireland	Saturday from Ireland
LONDON (Euston)........dep	6 5 p.m.		BELFAST (Donegall Quay)........dep		9 0 p.m.	11 0 p.m.
LIVERPOOL (Lime St.)........dep	9 40 p.m.		LIVERPOOL (Landing Stage) arr		6 30 a.m.	8 0 a.m.
(Landing Stage or) Princes Dock) } ..dep	10 15 p.m.		" (Lime St.)......dep		8 15 a.m.	9 30 a.m.
BELFAST (Donegall Quay)......arr	7 30 a.m.		LONDON (Euston)............arr		12 0 noon	1 45 p.m.

Passengers embarking at Liverpool should apply to the Belfast Steamship Co. (for Belfast), Royal Liver Building, Liverpool, (Telegraphic Address:—"Ladyships, Liverpool") in advance for berths.

Passengers embarking at Belfast should book berths and obtain berth tickets from the Belfast Steamship Co., 9, Donegall Place, Belfast (Telegraphic Address: "Passengers, Belfast"), and at Dublin from the British and Irish Steam Packet Co., 16, Westmoreland Street, Dublin (Telegraphic Address:—"Ladyships, Dublin").

Direct connections at Belfast with trains to all parts of Antrim, Derry, and Donegal.

ROYAL MAIL SERVICE.
Via HOLYHEAD and KINGSTOWN.
Through Bookings between all the Principal Stations in England and Ireland.

FASTEST AND BEST PASSENGER ROUTE.

TO IRELAND	LONDON (Euston) Depart	DUBLIN (Westland Row) Arrive	FROM IRELAND	DUBLIN (Westland Row) Depart	LONDON (Euston) Arrives
MORNING SERVICE.			**MORNING SERVICE.**		
EACH WEEK DAY.......	8045 a.m.	6 0 p	DAILY, except Sats.& Suns	8 45 a.m.	5 50 p.m.
SATURDAYS ONLY.......	1 0 p.m.	10 35 p	SATURDAYS ONLY.........	8 35 a.m.	5 32 p.m.
SATS. July 24th to Sept 11 incl.	8 50 a.m.	6 39 p	SATS., July 30th only.......	11215 a.m.	9 6 p.m.
				1 10 p.m.	1 1 p.m.
EVENING SERVICE.			**EVENING SERVICE.**		
			EACH WEEK NIGHT.......	8 10 p.m.	5630 a.m.
WEEKLY.........	8845 a.m.	6845 a	FRIS, July 29 to Aug. 26th	7 50 p.m.	5 15 a.m.
FRIDAY, July 29th only.......	1 20 a.m.	1 15 p			
			SUNDAYS.		
FRIDAY ONLY (except July 29th or Sept. 9th).......	10 15 p.m.	3 2 a	July 24th to Sept 11th incl.	8 25 a.m.	7 10 p.m.
			Every Sunday.........	8 22 p.m.	5 30 a.m.

1st & 3rd class Sleeping lins on night trains.

‡ On July 29th conveys Sleeping Car Passengers only. Passengers depart London (Eus.) 8 30 p.m. Passengers occupying Sleeping Accommodation on the Boat may occupy their berths on arrival at Holyhead off the 5 20 p.m. train (Week Days) from Euston, arriving Holyhead 11 30 §, and 4 15 p.m. train (Sundays) from Euston, arriving Holyhead 12 15 midnight. § Passengers may remain on board the Steamer at Kingstown, and so obtain a full night's sleep, afterwards travelling by the 7 45 a.m. (Week Days) from Kingstown, arriving Westland Row 8 2 a.m., and § (Sundays) from Kingstown, arriving Westland Row 8 25 a. ¶ Passengers may remain on board the Steamer at Dunlaoghaire (Sun. morns. excepted), and so obtain a full night's sleep, afterwards travelling by the 7 20 a.m. (Week Days) from Holyhead, due Euston 1 10 p.m. ⊙ On Sats., also Fridays, July 22nd to Aug. 12th inclusive, dep. 8 30 a.m. ‡ Will not apply on July 29th after September 10th.

APPLICATIONS AND CHARGES FOR CABINS:—
Applications for accommodation on the Steamers from Ireland should be addressed to Irish Traffic Manager, 15, Westmoreland Street, Dublin, and for accommodation on the Steamers from Eng., to the Marine Superintendent, Holyhead. Special Make Rooms....... 15s. 9d. Including over Deck Berths in Cabins and open Berths free. Evening Deck Cabins....... 8s. 0d. "made-up" Berth charge of 2s. 9d. each Berth if "made-up" bed provided. Main Deck Cabins....... 3s. 0d.

ROYAL MAIL AND SHORTEST SEA ROUTE.
Via STRANRAER and LARNE.
The Services between CARLISLE and BELFAST are given on Week-days only, and until further notice will be as follows :—

To IRELAND	a.m.	†A p.m.	*A p.m.	From IRELAND	a.m.	A p.m.
				Belfast, York Rd. (Train)dep.	9 33	6125
LONDON (Euston)............dep	10 5	8 0	8 30	Larne Harbour (Ship)......	10B15	7 15
	p.m.	a.m.	a.m.			a.m.
Carlisle (Train)...............	4 12	3 53	3 13	Stranraer Harbour " ....arr.	12 15	9 10
Stranraer Harbour (Ship)....	7 0	6 56	5 0			a.m.
Larne Harbour ....arr.	9 10	8 20	8 20	Carlisle ....dep.	3C21	12 33
Belfast, York Road (Train)...arr.	9 50	8 58	8 58	LONDON (Euston)......arr.	3C35	7 30
				(St. Pancras)......		9 20

A 1st & 3rd class Sleeping accommodation, London (Euston) to Stranraer Harbour and vice versa.
B On Saturdays dep. 10 10 a.m. C Arrives Carlisle 3 5 a.m. † Except Saturday and Sunday Nights, Sunday and Monday Mornings.
* Except Saturday and Sunday Nights, Sunday and Monday Mornings. ‡ Except Sunday nights.
* Sunday Nights and Monday Mornings only.
A Restaurant Car is attached to the 9-17 p.m. train from Stranraer to Glasgow which runs in connection with the 6-55 p.m. service from Belfast.

For Train Services and connections with this route, see pages 756, 758, 759, and 1119a.
Applications for Berths on the Steamer from Stranraer should be addressed to the Station Master, Stranraer Harbour. Tel. Address: "Shortsea, Stranraer."

These Services are subject to Material Alteration or discontinuance without further notice and the Companies will not be responsible for any Loss, Injury, or Delay through any failure to afford these Services or any Modified Service. For further information see the Railway Companies' Time Tables.

◄◄ As this advertisement demonstrates, the LMS also provided boat trains for the British & Irish ferry services from Liverpool to Dublin, and those from the same port operated by the Belfast Steamship Company. (Bradshaw)

◄ Looking much used, one of the Heysham–Belfast ferries was the *Duke of Argyll*, seen here alongside a quay in northern France while operating as a hospital ship during the Second World War.

Clyde. The Highland Railway had a port at the Kyle of Lochalsh, while the Portpatrick & Wigtownshire Joint Railway had its important port at Stranraer.

The LMS also inherited several canals, with more than 540 miles altogether of which more than 490 miles were in England. Unlike the docks and ferry services, these

➤ A Fowler 'Dock Tank', designed for working on dockside lines and shunting yards, with a short wheelbase to ensure that tight curves could be negotiated and a substantial end overhang so a larger boiler could be used. (HMRS)

lacked any real potential for growth and it was to be a case of managed decline.

Holyhead had services to Kingstown and Dublin North Wall, although at the time of Grouping the latter had its passenger services suspended – a throwback to economies made during the First World War – but still carried cattle and cargo. Holyhead also had the service to Greenore, supported by the Dundalk, Newry & Greenore Railway's services in Ireland. There were services from both Fleetwood and Heysham to

Belfast, and from Liverpool to Drogheda. This network of routes was augmented by the service between Stranraer and Larne, the shortest crossing to Ireland, but still a lengthy journey for those from the north-west of England.

Thanks to the LYR, the LMS had services from Goole on the River Humber to Dunkirk, Ghent, Antwerp, Rotterdam, Amsterdam, Hamburg and Copenhagen, but these were all mainly general cargo services. Goole never reached the size of its neighbours Hull and Grimsby, but a joint service existed with the LNER for passengers to Zeebrugge from Hull.

There were also the railway steamers on the Firth of Clyde, on Loch Lomond, Loch Tay and Loch Awe, as well as on Lake Windermere and Coniston Water. Ferries included those between Tilbury and Gravesend, Heysham and Fleetwood, and the Kyleakin ferry. The Clyde steamers were operated through a subsidiary which had been part of the Caledonian Railway's dowry for the LMS: the Caledonian Steam Packet Company, one of the predecessors of today's Caledonian McBrayne.

The company rationalised itself in 1928 by concentrating its passenger routes to Belfast on Heysham, and transferred its services to the Isle of Man to the Isle of Man Steam Packet Company. The previous year, the LMS introduced a boat train to Tilbury for a service to Dunkirk operated by the Angleterre-Lorraine-Alsace Company.

St Pancras was the major terminus for the LMS boat trains connecting with the main ocean liner routes of the day. Between July and the end of September these totalled 105 between St Pancras and Tilbury, while between Euston and Liverpool there were another 80. The boat trains in question were for the Cunard liners, sailing for the

Did you know?

The war years were marked not just by bomb damage, but also by neglect due to the shortage of materials and manpower, even though women were called up for war service on the railways. Cleaning was one job that was frequently neglected, to the extent that locomotives had to have their numbers chalked on the sides as the sign-written numerals were masked by dirt. Passengers had to open doors to see at which station the train had stopped. One wit scrawled the graffito in the dirt:

'The LMS – A hell of a mess!'

United States and Canada from Liverpool; those bound for Tilbury were for P&O and the Orient Line sailing to India, the Far East and Australia.

While the LMS commissioned new ships for its services, it also improved the ports, including a ramp at Stranraer in Scotland for the first British drive-on/drive-off ferries.

At Heysham in 1928 the LMS introduced three new ships, all sister ships (i.e. ships of the same class) of 3,600grt: *Duke of Argyll*, *Duke of Lancaster* and *Duke of Rothesay*. In 1935 a fourth ship, *Duke of York*, was commissioned.

Between Stranraer and Larne, the tradition was for the ships to be named after princesses. The most important ship the LMS introduced on this route was the *Princess Victoria*, Britain's first drive-on/drive-off car ferry when she entered service in 1939. She was requisitioned by the

◄ The LMS were among the pioneers of domestic air services in the British Isles and their operations were only brought to a halt by the Second World War. This is a de Havilland Rapide, loading air cargo. (*LMS Magazine*)

Admiralty in December and sunk by an enemy mine the following year.

At Holyhead the LMS inherited no less than six modern ships – *Curraghmore*, *Anglia*, *Hibernia*, *Cambria*, *Scotia* and *Slieve Donard* – all commissioned by the LNWR between 1919 and 1921, largely to replace wartime losses, so the LMS did not need to provide any new tonnage on this route.

Despite the heavy investment in shipping and ports, the railways were among the pioneers of domestic air services in the British Isles, with their involvement starting in 1933. Initially, the more ambitious companies acted independently, but a combined operation, Railway Air Services (RAS), was formed in 1934 involving the LMS, as well as the GWR and the Southern. The LNER was not involved. Air services within Scotland were operated by Scottish Airways, which collaborated with RAS, as did the airlines operating to the Isle of Wight and the Channel Islands. The vice president in charge of scientific research at the LMS, Sir Harold Hartley, became the first chairman of RAS.

The railways realised that if they did not develop air transport, others would. Nevertheless, the LMS seemed far less interested in aviation than the GWR and the Southern, and was not involved when, in 1938, a new airline was formed by these companies, Great Western & Southern Air Services – despite RAS flying a million miles during the summer of 1937. Among the routes with LMS involvement was the Royal Mail service between London Croydon and Belfast, calling en route at Birmingham, Stoke and Liverpool, with two services daily in each direction during 1937, so that for the first time passengers could make an out and back daytrip.

From the beginning, the railways had found road transport important, but they were only allowed to operate goods vehicles and buses to and from goods depots or railway stations. On its formation, the LMS had 9,100 horses for its cartage operations, and 1,350 road vehicles.

The intention was to protect existing operators and not allow an extension of the railway monopoly. Nevertheless, the railways felt that road transport had an unfair advantage as it did not have the heavy fixed costs of track, signalling systems, stations, depots and works that the railways had.

From 1929 the railways were allowed to buy or invest in bus operators or road haulage firms. In the case of bus services, their own operations had to be sold to established operators, so the LMS and other railway companies sometimes used their existing services and vehicles as payment for a share in an established company.

While two railway companies would sometimes jointly invest in a bus company that operated across the boundary between their areas of operations, most often the railways acted individually in acquiring bus companies. As they often collaborated on the handling of freight traffic, it was not surprising that when they eventually did move into road haulage in 1933, they did so jointly, with the Big Four acquiring Carter Patterson, the parcels specialist, and Pickfords, the removals specialist. Another reason for operating jointly was that road haulage was even more fragmented than bus operation, with few haulage operators having a nationwide presence.

In September 1929 the LMS revealed that it had entered into agreements with

thirty-six bus companies operating in England and Wales, and with the Scottish Motor Transport Company (SMTC), a group that owned many of the larger Scottish bus companies; these mainly operated rural and inter-urban services, although the smaller towns were also served by companies, leaving just Aberdeen, Dundee, Edinburgh and Glasgow with municipal operations.

In Scotland, along with the SMTC, the LMS was involved in Ayrshire Pullman and Gourock Pullman Services. The list in England and Wales included the Birmingham & Midland Motor Omnibus

106

Did you know?

The LMS was the leading British railway for services to Ireland, serving the Irish Republic from Holyhead and Northern Ireland from Heysham and Stranraer. Through railway services using train ferries were not possible because the Irish standard gauge was fixed at 5ft 3in against the British standard of 4ft 8½in. The LMS used its standard rolling stock for the Northern Counties Committee but fitted with broad-gauge bogies.

Company (BMMO), more usually known as Midland Red; Crosville Motor Services; Cumberland Motor Services; East Midland Motor Services; Eastern National Omnibus Company; Hebble Omnibus Services; Holyhead Motor Services, trading as Mona-Maroon; Lincolnshire Road Car Company; Llandudno Coaching & Carriage Company; North Western Road Car Company; Ortona Motor Company; Peterborough Electric Traction Company; Ribble Motor Services; Trent Motor Traction Company; Yorkshire Traction Company; and the Yorkshire (Woollen District) Electric Tramways Company. The LMS was also involved jointly in bus services operated by the local authorities in Sheffield, Leeds and Halifax.

Especially in Northern Ireland, some of the rural bus services were used to replace or reduce loss-making railway services.

In an attempt to provide a through road and rail service on little-used branch lines, in 1932 the LMS tried out the 'Ro-Railer', a French concept. In 1934, three modifications of standard four-wheel, forty-seat buses were supplied to the LMS by Leyland. While these had basic buffers and drawgear, they lacked the power to pull a trailer.

◄ The LMS pursued the concept of the 'Ro-Railer', a bus that could drop or retract its railway wheels and thereby run on the road or on tracks. French prototypes were tested before this Leyland bus was tried. (*LMS Magazine*)

In common with the other railway companies, the LMS remained in private ownership throughout the Second World War, but was controlled and directed by the Railway Executive Committee. Initially, speed restrictions were imposed and frequencies cut, while journey times lengthened. The speed restrictions were eventually eased and the reduced frequencies were suspended – following public protest – until new reduced frequencies could be introduced. Night sleepers were largely reserved for those travelling on government business, first class was withdrawn in the London suburban area, and trains lost their catering facilities.

As an example of the reduced frequencies and lengthened journey times, the service from Euston and St Pancras to Glasgow was cut from twelve trains in 1938 to six in 1939. The average journey time was increased from eight hours, six minutes to ten hours, four minutes, but the fastest journey in October 1938 had taken just six hours, thirty minutes for the 401 miles.

Many of the company's ships were requisitioned to help move and support the British Expeditionary Force in France, and among the losses was the roll-on/roll-off ferry *Princess Victoria*.

The LMS helped in the evacuation of children and nursing mothers from the major cities, including not only London, but Birmingham, Manchester and Glasgow.

Inevitably, the LMS suffered from the intense German bombing of 1940–41. It was particularly badly affected by the air raid on Coventry on the night of 14/15 November 1940, with no less than 122 bombs exploding on its lines around the city. Traffic between Euston and Birmingham had to be diverted at Rugby

➤ The signalman was essential to the safe running of the railway. The LMS enhanced its signalling system by adopting the Midland Railway's control centres so there was an overall co-ordinating function. (HMRS)

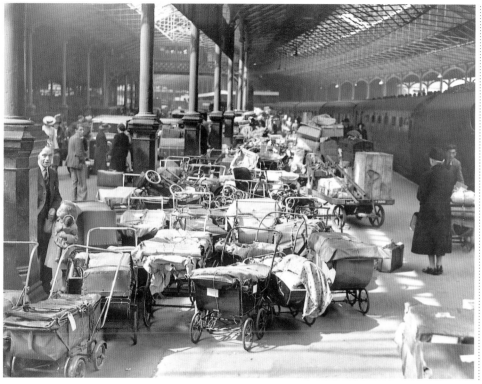

◄◄ This locomotive has a box on the front so its performance can be monitored. A plan with the LNER to establish a major British testing facility ended with the outbreak of war. (HMRS)

◄ The railways made possible the mass evacuation of children from industrial areas on the eve of war in 1939, but as the 'phoney war' dragged on, expectant mothers and children drifted back, as this photograph of Euston shows. (IWM HU82779)

Did you know?

The railways had long been able to run buses to and from their stations or to operate road haulage on the same basis, but it was not until 1929 that they were allowed to invest in road transport. Even so, from their formation in 1923 to the outbreak of the Second World War in 1939, they continued to campaign against what they saw as the unfair advantages enjoyed by road transport, which did not have the same overheads and responsibility for the infrastructure that burdened the railways. The general public felt that the railways protested too much!

and sent via Leamington and Kenilworth, returning to the main line at Berkswell. Nevertheless, within two days one platform was available at Coventry station, and the London to Birmingham trains returned to their usual route, using the Coventry avoiding line, a week after the raid.

For the LMS, the worst raid occurred on 10/11 May 1941, when a 1,000lb bomb shot through the roof of St Pancras, continued through the floor of the station, and buried itself in the London clay below, exploding some 25ft down. The explosion created a large crater at the concourse end of platforms 3 and 4, but even more seriously, it destroyed about 20ft of the tunnel carrying the Metropolitan Line and the Midland trains to the city. Clearing up the mess and initiating repairs was made difficult by the presence of an unexploded bomb halfway along No. 2 platform.

Nevertheless, undamaged platforms were used and within seven days, with the exception of two platforms, all lines were working again.

The war saw the company's building and repair facilities largely taken over for the production of armaments; this, combined with the conscription of many employees and a shortage of materials, resulted in a railway that was considerably rundown when peace returned. Post-war restrictions on materials and delays in releasing railwaymen from the armed forces meant that it was not possible for the LMS to become its former self before nationalisation on 1 January 1948.

➤ 'Small locomotive' Midland also built and operated the Lickey banker, the massive 0-10-0 'decapod', needed to assist heavy trains up this gradient in the West Midlands. (HMRS)

1 & 2) As they were on the same main line and affected the same trains, taken together are Shap Incline – with a gradient between 1 in 147 and 1 in 75 as the line rises 885ft in 31½ miles running northward – and Beattock Bank, with a gradient between 1 in 88 and 1 in 74 to a summit of 1,015ft. These peaks posed a massive challenge to steam locomotives, regardless of whether they were hauling a heavy express or an even heavier, but slower, goods train. The situation was bad whether the train was heading north or south, as in between lay Carlisle, which was almost at sea level, where there was often a locomotive or even a crew change. On the downhill stretches, speeds of 90mph were often attained.

3) The Settle & Carlisle line, just 72 miles in length but with thirteen tunnels and twenty-one viaducts, of which the longest is the Ribblehead Viaduct. The line is steeply graded with much of the line from Settle at 1 in 100 for the first 15 miles and running at more than 1,000ft above sea level for much of its length.

4) The Lickey Incline between Bromsgrove and Blackwell, with northbound trains facing a gradient of 1 in 37.75 for 2 miles. Only the shortest of trains could manage the slope without banking assistance, and for the incline the Midland Railway broke away from its policy of small locomotives and in 1920 built the UK's only decapod, or 0-10-0, numbered 2290.

6221

116

▲ Locomotives built without streamlining were known as the Duchess class, but not all were named after duchesses. This is the *City of Birmingham*, after nationalisation and even electrification! (HMRS)

◀ This is what a Coronation without cladding looked like: here is *Queen Elizabeth* after the streamlining had been removed. Many believe this was a far more attractive styling than the streamlining. (HMRS)

GO BY RAIL WITH A
CHEAP
"MONTHLY RETURN"

That's the Ticket!

Cheap "Monthly Return" Tickets are issued all the year round between most stations and are available by any train any day.

Full particulars from any Railway Station Office or Agency

G.W.R   LMS   L·N·E·R   S.R

▲ Cheap return fares were another joint marketing campaign. Fares could be as low as a penny a mile. (Railway Companies Association)

◄◄ The Coronation class was the most powerful steam locomotive on Britain's railways. This is No. 6229 *Duchess of Hamilton* before she was rebuilt with streamlining and put on show at the National Railway Museum. (Optimist on the Run, Wikimedia Commons)

◄ For many, Stanier will be best remembered for his famous Class 5MT 4-6-0, the famous Black 5. This is No. 45407 (the post-nationalisation number) on a visit to the North Yorkshire Moors Railway. (Author)

5) Stanier's Duchess-class locomotives were the most powerful steam engines on Britain's railways, with the first examples in 1937 having heavily streamlined casings somewhat reminiscent of US designs. Most, however, were built without streamlining after 1938, and the streamlining was later removed from all locomotives. These impressive locomotives were sometimes claimed to be capable of exceeding *Mallard*'s speed record, but this was never put to the test. Even so, No. 6220 Coronation reached 114mph on a special run.

6) Stanier's 'Turbomotive', No. 6202, completed in 1935 at Crewe, was based on the Princess Royal class, and despite being heavier than a Princess, showed slightly better economy. The idea was to see whether a steam turbine, as used in ships, would be superior to the pistons, cylinders and connecting rods of a conventional steam locomotive. Experience showed that although she was a powerful and free-running unit, much special attention was needed and she was scrapped in 1952.

7) The Black 5s, or Stanier Class 5 4-6-0 mixed traffic locomotives, were based on the GWR's Hall class, but with differences such as outside Walschaerts valve gear, and became one of the most outstanding steam locomotives ever. They were used throughout the LMS and after nationalisation British Railways distributed them far and wide, as well as basing a standard 4-6-0 on the Black 5.

1829	The Rainhill Trials discover the best locomotives for the Liverpool & Manchester Railway.
1830	Liverpool & Manchester Railway opens – the earliest of the LMS predecessor companies.
1837	Grand Junction Railway opens throughout.
1843	Grand Junction Railway opens Crewe works.
1844	Midland Railway forms through the amalgamation of Birmingham & Derby Junction, Midland Counties and North Midland Railways.
1846	London & North Western Railway forms through amalgamation of Grand Junction (including the Liverpool & Manchester), London & Birmingham and Manchester & Birmingham Railways.
1850	Route to Holyhead is completed with the opening of the Britannia Bridge over the Menai Strait.
1860	The first water pick-up apparatus is installed on the LNWR, ending the need for locomotives to stop to take on water.

◄ One problem for steam locomotives when it snowed was water freezing in the water troughs, which meant they had to stop to pick up water. (HMRS)

1869	First flyover is completed by the LNWR at Birdswood Junction.
1872	Midland Railway conveys third-class passengers by all trains.
1874	Midland Railway introduces the first Pullman cars to the UK.
1875	Midland Railway abolishes second class and admits third-class passengers to these carriages.
1885	LNWR and Caledonian Railway introduce a mail train between London and Aberdeen, but without passenger accommodation.
1888	First railway 'race to the north' between West and East Coast companies running day expresses between London and Edinburgh.
1890	Forth Bridge opens, with the Midland Railway as the biggest single contributor towards the cost of construction.
1895	Second railway 'race to the north' between West and East Coast companies running night expresses between London and Aberdeen. The West Coast companies win.

1914 The First World War begins and the government takes control of the railways; they remain in private ownership but are administered by the Railway Executive Committee.

1921 Government control of the railways ends. The Railways Act requires the formation of the Southern; Western; North West, Midland and West Scottish; and North Eastern, Eastern and East Scottish Railways.

1923 London, Midland & Scottish Railway (LMS) forms with constituent companies, including the London & North Western Railway, Lancashire & Yorkshire Railway, Midland Railway, Caledonian Railway and Glasgow & South Western Railway: in effect, the act's North West, Midland and West Scottish Railway.

1928 Third-class sleeping cars are introduced by LMS (and the LNER and GWR as well).

➤ Another snow scene; visibility looks as if it might be poor, especially for high-speed running. (HMRS)

1929 Railway Passenger Duty is abolished; the sums saved are to be capitalised and used for modernisation. Railways are allowed to buy road transport companies.

1937 LMS introduces the Coronation Scot streamlined express between Euston and Glasgow.

1939 The Second World War begins and the government takes control of the railways; they remain in private ownership but are administered by the Railway Executive Committee.

1946 The railways return to the control of the Big Four companies.

1947 The Transport Act sets up the British Transport Commission, preparing for the nationalisation of the four grouped railways, as well as railway-owned ports and road transport.

1948 LMS is nationalised and becomes part of British Railways, but divided between the London Midland Region and the Scottish Region; the Northern Counties Committee is eventually passed to the Ulster Transport Authority.

ARTICLES

LMS Magazine, November 1923 – December 1947
North Western Magazine, January – October 1923

BOOKS

Morrison, Gavin, *London Midland: Then and Now*, Ian Allan, 1995
Nash, G.G., *The LMS at War*, London, Midland & Scottish Railway, 1946
Nock, O.S., *A History of the LMS*, 3 vols, George Allen & Unwin, 1982–83
—, *The Railway Enthusiast's Encyclopaedia*, Hutchinson, 1968
Whitehouse, Patrick & St John Thomas, David, *LMS 150: The London,*
    Midland & Scottish Railway – A Century and a Half of Progress, 1987
Wragg, David, *The LMS Handbook 1923–1947*, Haynes, 2010
—, *A Historical Dictionary of the Railways of the British Isles*, Wharncliffe, 2009

WEBSITES

LMS Society: www.lmssociety.org.uk
National Railway Museum: www.nrm.org.uk

Other titles available in this series

DAVID WRAGG

THE STEAM LOCOMOTIVE STORY

■ ISBN 978 07524 8806 6

CHRIS FRAME & RACHELLE CROSS

THE QE2 STORY

■ ISBN 978 07524 5094 0

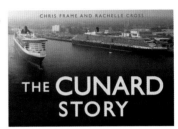

CHRIS FRAME AND RACHELLE CROSS

THE CUNARD STORY

■ ISBN 978 07524 5914 1

ROSA MATHESON

THE GWR STORY

■ ISBN 978 07524 5624 9

WILLIAM H. MILLER

THE GREAT LINERS STORY

■ ISBN 978 07524 6452 7

JOHN CHRISTOPHER

THE MARY ROSE STORY

■ ISBN 978 07524 6404 6

The History Press

Visit our website and discover thousands of other History Press books.
www.thehistorypress.co.uk